arranged & played

blues

for acoustic guitar

tablature & standard notation

solos

ISBN 978-0-7119-2789-6

HAL•LEONARD®

Copyright © 1998 by Wise Publications

Visit Hal Leonard Online at
www.halleonard.com

World headquarters, contact:
Hal Leonard
7777 West Bluemound Road
Milwaukee, WI 53213
Email: info@halleonard.com

In Europe, contact:
Hal Leonard Europe Ltd.
1 Red Place
London W1K 6PL
Email: info@halleonardeurope.com

In Australia, contact:
Hal Leonard Australia Pty. Ltd.
4 Lentara Court
Cheltenham, Victoria, 3192 Australia
Email: info@halleonard.com.au

PACK DESIGNED & ART DIRECTED BY MICHAEL BELL DESIGN.
BOOK DESIGN BY NICHE.
COMPILED BY PAT CONWAY.
MUSIC COMPILED AND PERFORMED BY JOHNNY NORRIS.
MUSIC PROCESSED BY SETON MUSIC GRAPHICS.
PHOTOGRAPHS COURTESY OF
LONDON FEATURES INTERNATIONAL, PICTORIAL PRESS,
VALERIE WILMER, CHARLYN ZLOTNIK.

PRINTED IN THE EU.

Striking Or Plucking The Strings

⊓ = Pick downwards with the plectrum.
V = Pick upwards with the plectrum.
p = Pluck downwards with your thumb.
i = Pluck upwards with your index finger.
m = Pluck upwards with your middle finger.
a = Pluck upwards with your ring finger.

Slide Going Up

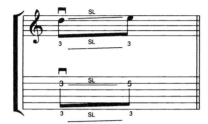

Strike the first note and slide up to the next.

Slide Coming Down

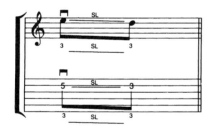

Strike the first note and slide down to the next.

Hammer-on

Sound a note as normal then hammer your LH finger down hard onto the next note to perform a hammer-on.

Pull-off

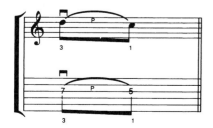

The pull-off is achieved by pulling your LH finger down off the string to create the next note.
P means pull-off.

**This piece combines 3 easy 'Riffs'
with 1 lick.**

By holding the "insurance notes" you can play a bit harder.
This is particularly useful if you're damping with the right hand or using a pick.

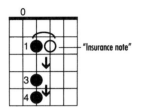
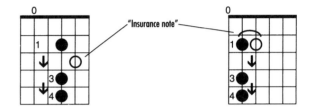

The 'A' Riff

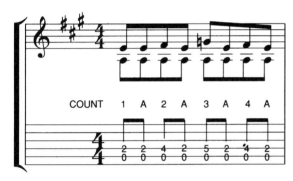

The 'D' Riff

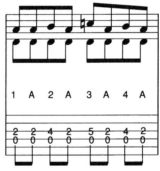

The 'E' Riff

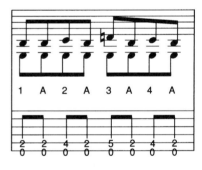

ROBERT CRAY

The Lick

1 Using any R.H. fingers play the notes slowly (but evenly).
  Leave out the slurs.
2 If you have any problems with the timing, count out loud.
  Tap your foot on each 1 or Trip.
3 Add one slur at a time. Make sure it is slow and even.
  Gradually speed up.

Box Pattern for lick

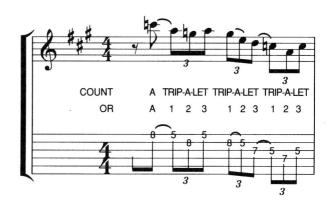

The Turnround

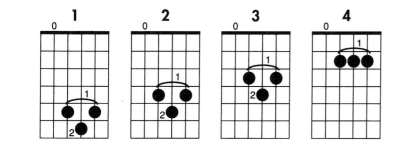

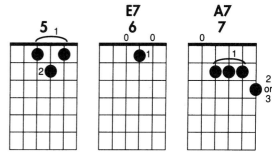

Bars 11 and 12 of a 12 bar blues are usually called the turnround.
The first time through the 'turnround' finishes on chord ⑥ which is E7.
This allows us to start the piece again.
The last time through the 'turnround' finishes on chord ⑦ which is A7.
Now the blues sounds finished.

SOHO BLUES

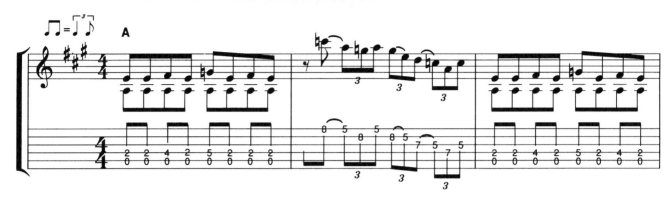

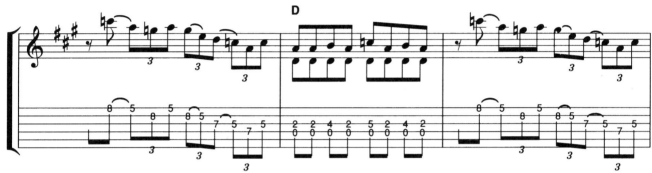

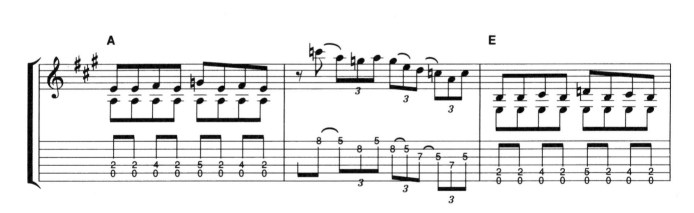

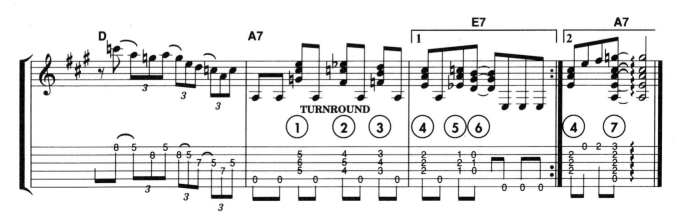

**This piece uses riffs only.
Once you've mastered the 'A' riff the
others ('E' and 'D') will be no problem.**

The 'A' Riff

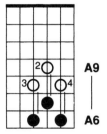

A9

A6

Keep your L.H. fingers pressed
down on the strings.
Let the A9 chord ring on.

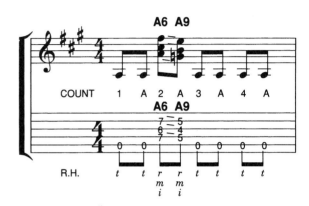

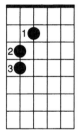

1. The slide from A9 up to A6 is
too fast to count.

2. $\frac{r}{m}$ Plays A9 but not A6.
   $\frac{r}{m}$ Plays A9 again on the way down.

3. For the triplet make sure
your 1st finger L.H. is in position.

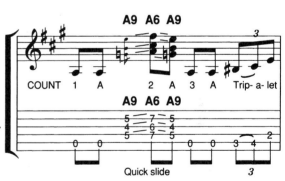

The 'D' Riff   The 'E' Riff

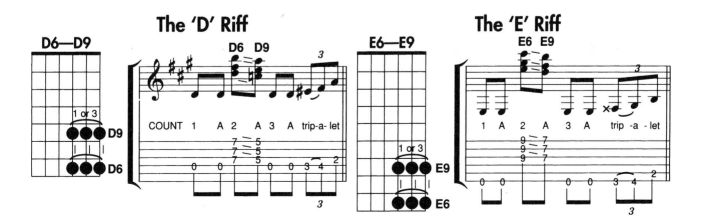

The Turnround

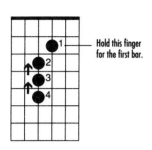

Hold this finger for the first bar.

COUNT 1 A trip-a-let trip-a-let trip-a-let | 1 A 2 A 3 A 4 A

R.H. *t t t i t t i t t i t t i t t i t t t t*

SHORTY (NIGHT)

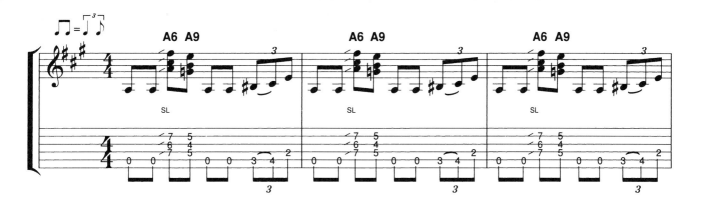

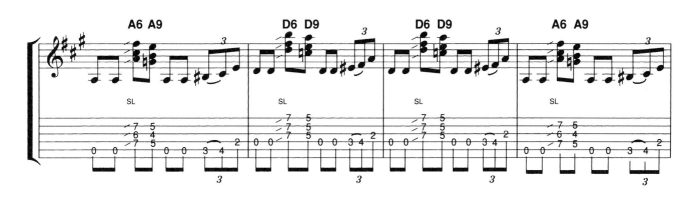

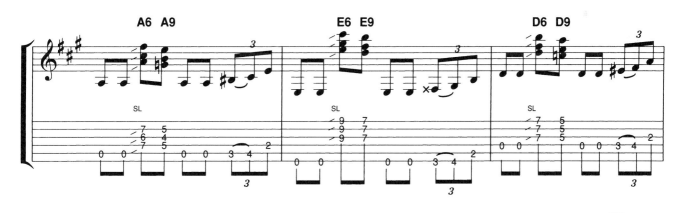

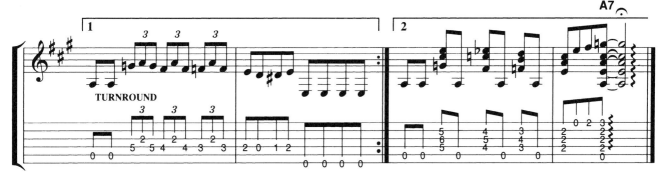

9

Preparation for
BAD BLOOD BLUES

This piece uses 3 riffs and 1 lick.
This time, though, in the key of 'E'.

The 'E' Riff

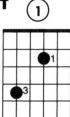 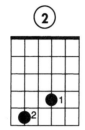 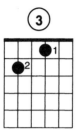

Keep 1st finger on 3rd string. It will act as a guide.

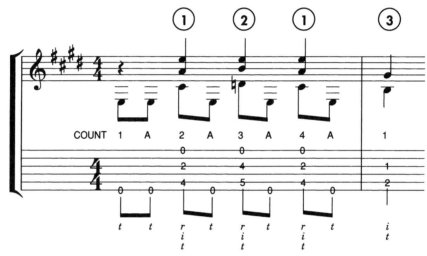

The Lick

1 Play slowly but evenly.
2 Count out loud as you play.
3 Tap foot on each 1.
4 Leave out the slurs at first if they cause difficulty.

There are many possible R.H. fingerings for this lick.
The one below is only a suggestion .
Experiment with different fingerings to find one
that is comfortable for you.

Box pattern

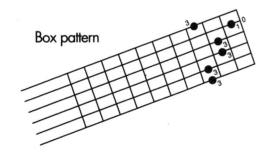

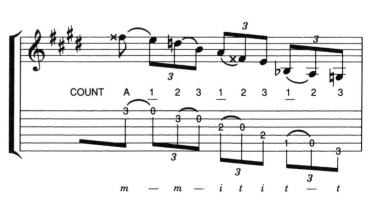

The lick in bar 8 leading to the B7 riff is slightly different,
but the count is the same.

The 'A' Riff

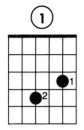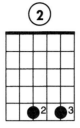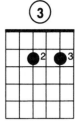

Use 2nd finger as a 'guide'

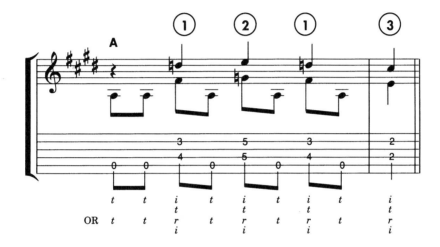

The 'B7' Riff

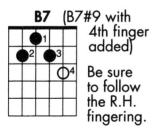

B7 (B7#9 with 4th finger added)

Be sure to follow the R.H. fingering.

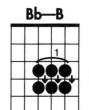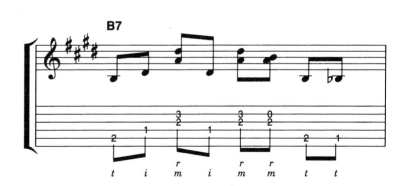

Shapes for the turnround

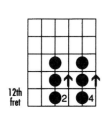

E

9th fret

Bb—B

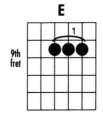

Slide the 1st finger up from 3rd to 4th fret

11

BAD BLOOD BLUES

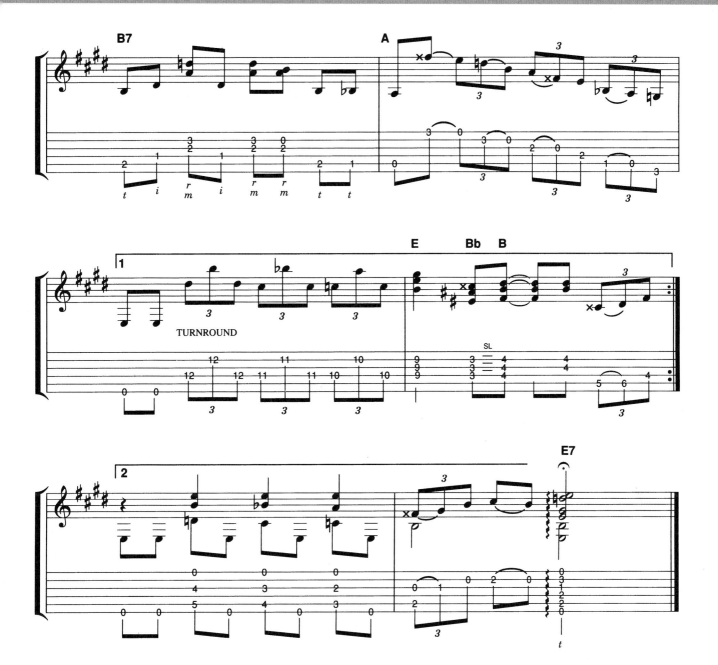

Lower the 6th string to D.
The 7th fret of the 6th string will now be
the same as the 5th string open.
The 6th string is now an octave
lower than the 4th string.

Note: The 3-note chords in the riffs
are neither major nor minor.

The 'D' Riff

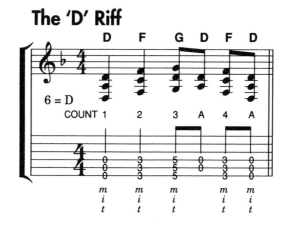

The 'G' Riff

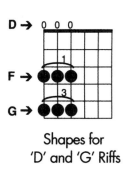

Shapes for
'D' and 'G' Riffs

The 'A' Riff

Shape for
the 'A' Riff

Box pattern for
licks 1, 2, 3 and 6

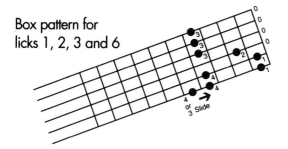

Hold this note as
long as possible
in licks 4 and 5

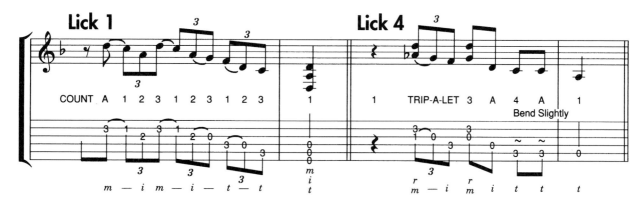

Lick 1

COUNT A 1 2 3 1 2 3 1 2 3 1

m — i m — i — t — t

Lick 4

TRIP-A-LET 3 A 4 A 1

Bend Slightly

r r
m — i m i t t t

The Final Chords

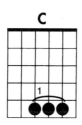

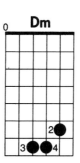

B.B. KING

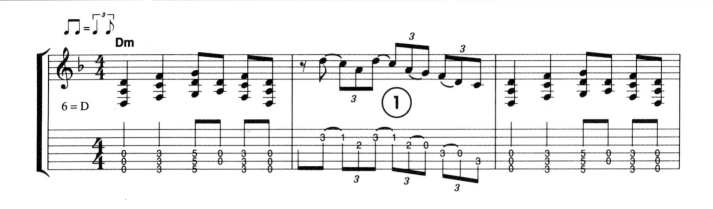

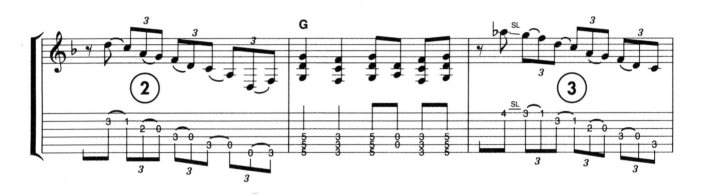

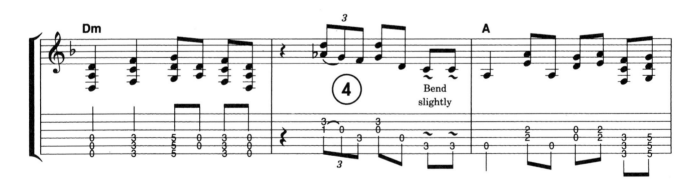

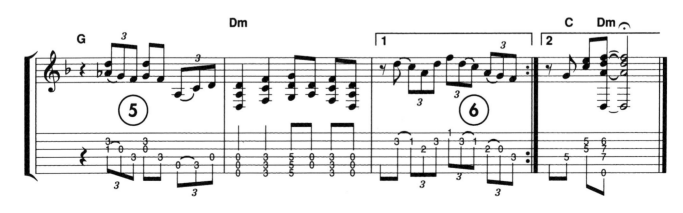

JUST ANOTHER WINE BAR

This is the last of the Riff/Lick pieces.
Bars 4–6 and 7–10 consist mainly of licks.

Box pattern for "A" Riff

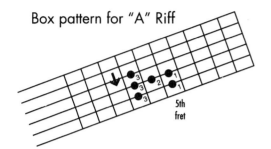

Tilt your 3rd finger over from the 4th string onto the 2nd and 3rd strings.
When you've hammered-on your 2nd finger leave it on.

Building Up The 'A' Riff — Part I

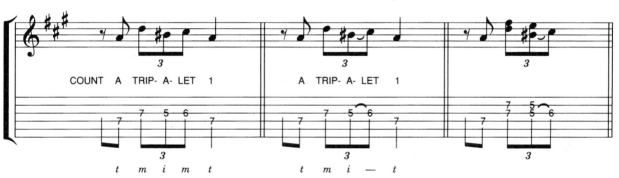

Adding the Hammer-On   Adding the Small Barrés

Part II

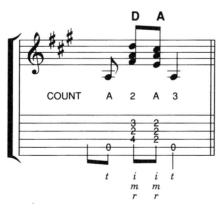

Leave barré on throughout this section.

Putting the riff together

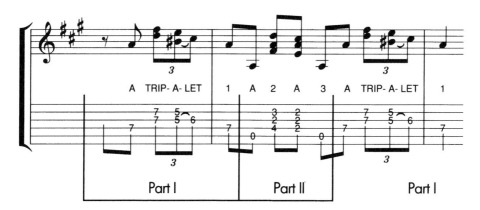

A TRIP-A-LET   1   A   2   A   3   A   TRIP-A-LET   1

Part I   Part II   Part I

The final chord

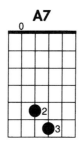

A7

The Turnround is the same as 'Cold Comfort.'

MUDDY WATERS

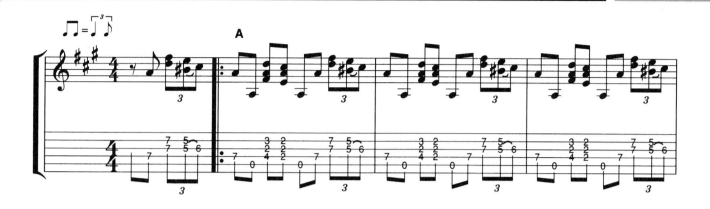

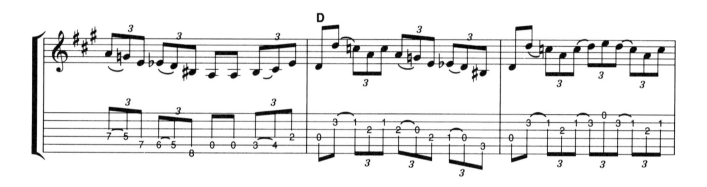

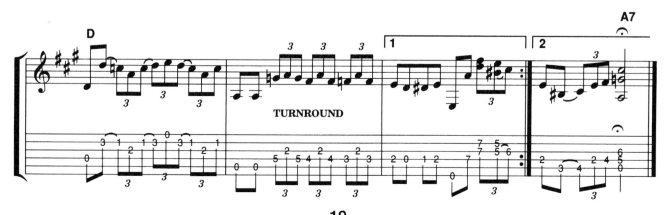

Alternating Bass — Fingerpicking

In this style of fingerpicking the object is to sound like two guitars.
The thumb plays a steady bass line of 4 notes to the bar.
The fingers play a melody on top of this.
Sounds easy—but it isn't!

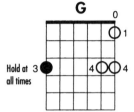

Here's a simple bass line in G. Hold the shape above.

No sweat. Now here's a simple melody. Hold the shape given.
Keep it slow and count along as you play.

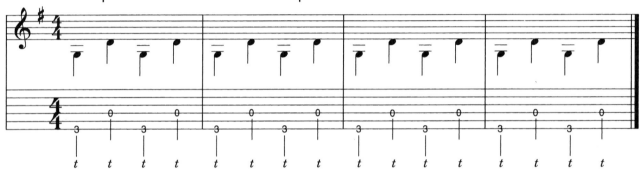

Simple! Now let's try putting the two parts together.
Take a deep breath.

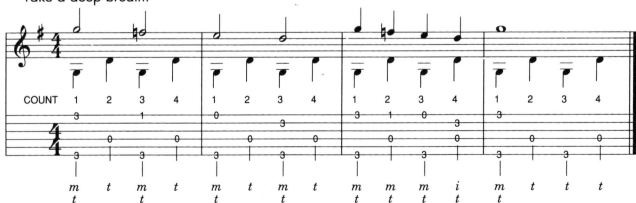

20

So far all the melody notes have been on the beat. Now we'll syncopate the melody.
The circled notes have been moved back half a beat. This adds more swing to the piece.

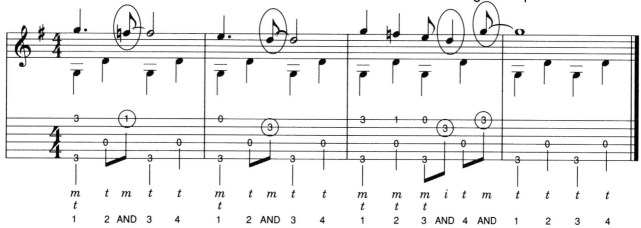

We can also move notes forward and add some open strings to the melody.

Some of these one bar picking patterns are very useful and can be used repeatedly.
Let's take the pattern in bar 2 above and play it over some chord changes.

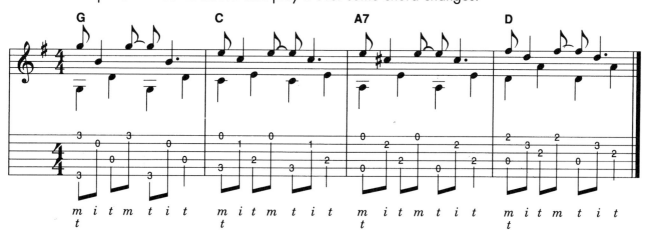

G

G (and G7)

Lift 4th finger at X.

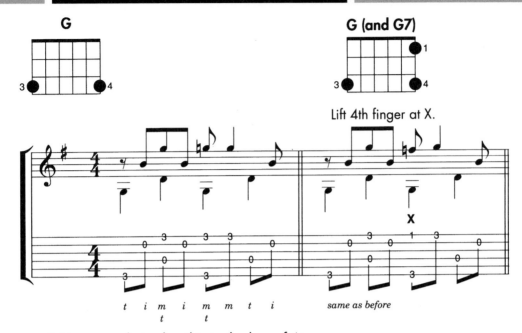

same as before

Using the same R.H. pattern let's play this in the key of A.

A (and A7)

Lift 4th finger at X

A

G# ↓ A

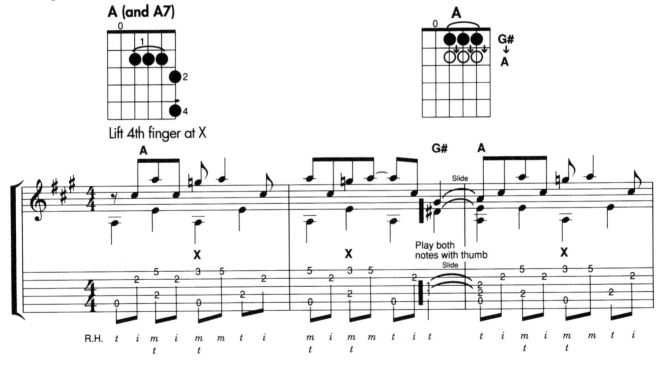

D (and D7)   **E (and E7)**

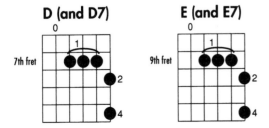

7th fret   9th fret

Note: With 4th finger on we have A, E and D
With 4th finger off we have A7, E7 and D7
For the 'E' and 'D' sections simply move the 'A' chord shape up the finger board.
The R.H. pattern doesn't change.

22

STEADY PICKIN'

ERIC CLAPTON

This uses a similar R.H. pick to the previous piece.
The rhythm is straight.
Count 1 <u>and</u> 2 <u>and</u>, instead of 1 A 2 A etc.

New chords needed for 'Southern Rag'

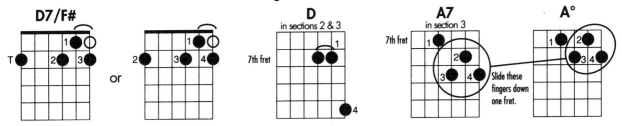

D7/F#   or   D
in sections 2 & 3
7th fret

A7
in section 3
7th fret   Slide these fingers down one fret.

A°

The final run in C is a version of the famous 'Flatt Run' used by all Bluegrass players.
You can try it with or without slurs.

With slurs: Without slurs: (pay attention to R.H. fingers)

NEIL YOUNG

25

SOUTHERN RAG

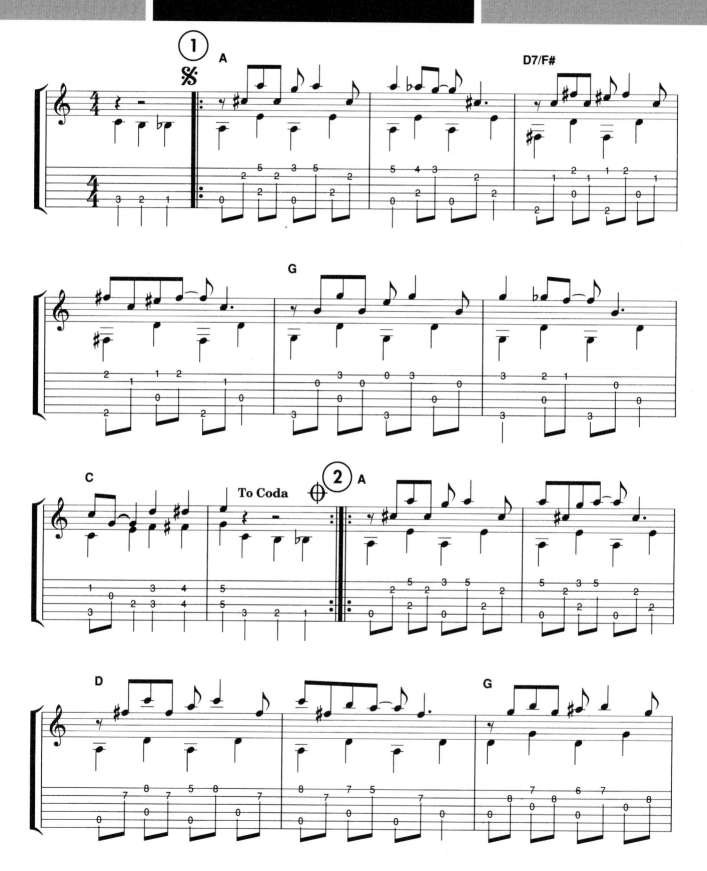

27

Off Beat Chord Changes

Play this pattern slowly but evenly.

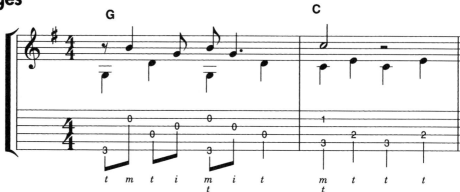

Now let's syncopate the melody by moving the 'c' note in bar two back half a beat.
Make sure you change to the C chord where indicated.
The melody note should ring on into the second bar.

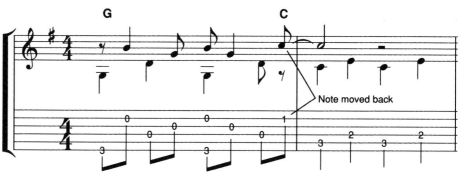

Note moved back

If the encircled parts cause a problem here are three ways to tackle it.

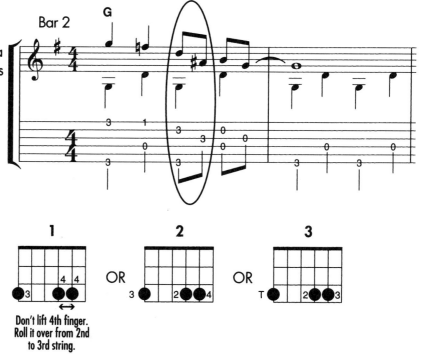

1

Don't lift 4th finger.
Roll it over from 2nd to 3rd string.

OR

2

OR

3

Bar 1
This is also
the shape
needed for
bar 3.

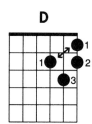

Bar 2
Slide the barré
from the first fret
to the 2nd fret.
This occurs in
each bar of A.

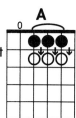

Bars 7 and 15

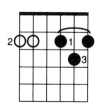

This is how I play it.   This is more
practical on
a wide necked
guitar.

Off-beat slurs — Bar 3

First try this bar without
the slur as written below.

Now add the slur. Make sure
not to drop the thumb note.

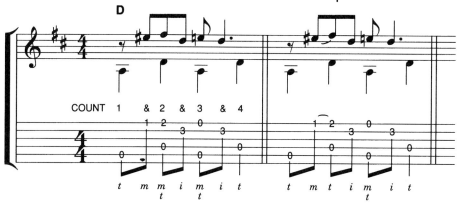

Here's a slightly different way of playing bars 9 and 11 using a slide or
hammer-on instead of a bend.
This is more suitable for a nylon string guitar.

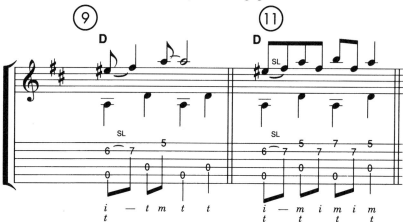

LOST KEY BLUES

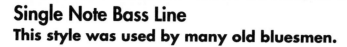
Single Note Bass Line
This style was used by many old bluesmen.

First play the melody as indicated without the bass line. Slide the shape up from one fret below each time you start the triplet.

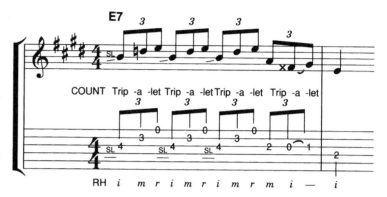

Now add the thumb on each beat. ie. each trip in the count. Note: hold the last note in Bar 1 (G#) into the 2nd bar.

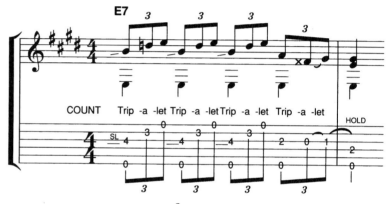

Where the melody is less busy we can play two thumb notes per beat. Where the triplet occurs drop the 2nd bass note.

You also need these shapes during the piece.

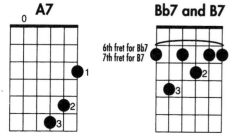

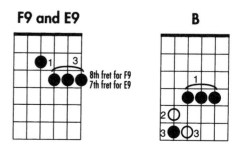

Check the right hand in bars 9 and 10.

33

Knowing which box you're in is crucial here.

Box
Pattern 1

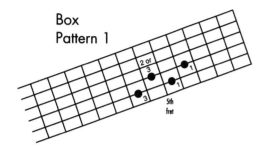

Box
Pattern 2

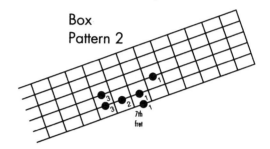

The 'B' chord shape for line 3 bar 2

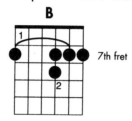

If the rhythm causes any problems try 'unsyncopating' the melody to begin with.
Here's the first three bars 'unsyncopated', compare them to the first three bars in the piece.

DOWN IN THE DELTA

Preparation for
BAR ROOM BLUES

**This piece is based on a modern 'Urban Blues' lick.
To get the timing right listen to the recording.
Here are the boxes and chord shapes you need.**

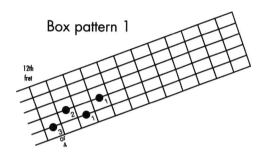

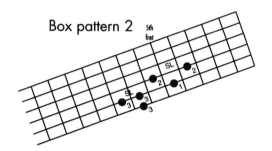

Chord shapes required for bars 9, 10, 12, 13

C9, F9, E9

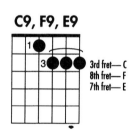

3rd fret— C
8th fret— F
7th fret— E

B9

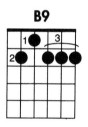

B

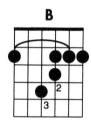

**9th chords are commonly used in blues. They often replace 7th chords.
Notice how they often move chromatically e.g. C9—B9 and F9—E9.**

Shapes for the turnround

1

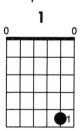

2

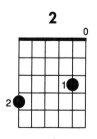

3

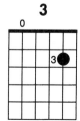

4

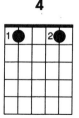

BAR ROOM BLUES

Not all blues have 12 bars.
Many blues pieces have 8 or 16 bars.
This 8 bar blues uses some 'modern' sounding chords at the end.

A "Traditional" 8 Bar Blues.

E   B   E   A

| / / / / | / / / / | / / / / | / / / / |

E   B7   E   B

| / / / / | / / / / | / / / / | / / / / |

└——— TURNROUND ———┘

8 Bar Blues with 'substitution chords'.

E   B   E   A

| / / / / | / / / / | / / / / | / / / / |

E   C#7   F#7   B7   E   B

| / / / / | / / / / | / / / / | / / / / |

└——— TURNROUND ———┘

B

7th fret

C#7

F#7(b9)

Apart from the chords there are two box positions needed.

Box Pattern 1

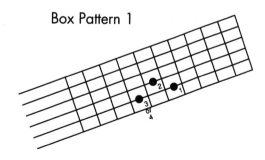

Box Pattern 2

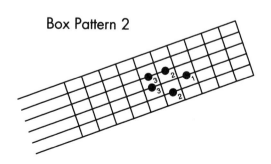

EIGHT BARS ON THE HIGHWAY

Rolls are a subtle but effective way to add 'swing' to a piece.

The roll for this piece is:

$$t \quad i \quad \overset{r}{m} \quad t \quad i \quad \overset{r}{m} \quad t$$

1 AND 2 AND 3 AND 4

Notice where the *t*'s are — on 1, the AND between 2 and 3, and on 4.

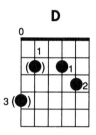

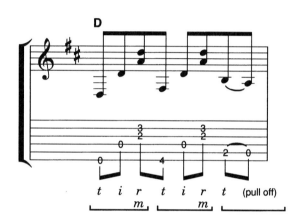

If you're not used to slurring (Hammer-Ons and Pull-Offs)
the licks in this piece will give you something to work on.
Watch for the R.H. fingerings as well.
Here are three examples.
The others should cause no problem once you've mastered these.

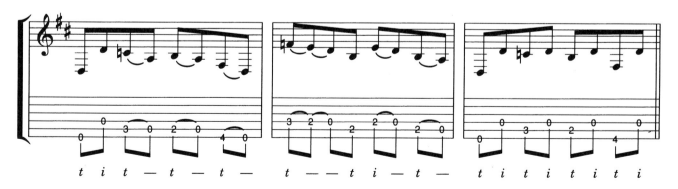

ROLLIN' HOME

RY COODER

More Rolls

This time the pattern extends over two bars.
Try this pattern on a 'G' and 'A' chord— $|\ t\ i\ m\ t\ i\ m\ t\ i\ |\ m\ t\ i\ m\ |$
Result: Instant "Big Band" sound.

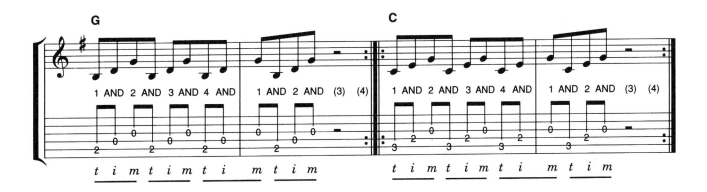

The pattern in "Overdrivin" is very similar to this

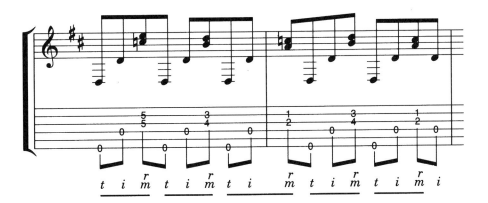

Notice how each bunch of 3 *(t i ʳm)* relates to the count.

OVERDRIVIN'

MEAN STREET

This last tune uses all the techniques covered in the book.

Single Note Bass

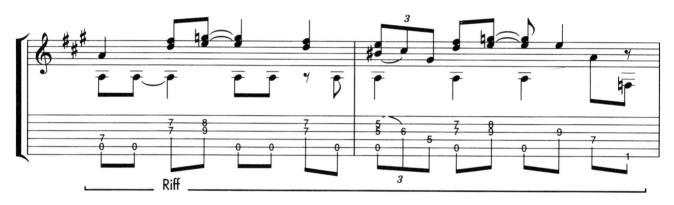

Riff

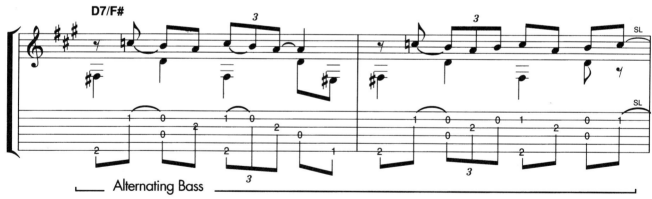

Alternating Bass

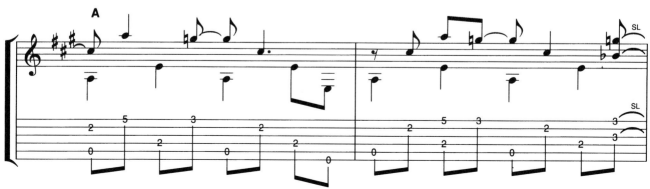

46